AF241469

Ultimate Youth Life Style

The guides to achieve a lifestyle in times of youth

Yaxuan Elsa Yang

Library of Congress Control Number: 2022912658

PAPERBACK: 978-1-957575-74-2
EBOOK: 978-1-957575-75-9

Ordering Information:

For orders and inquiries, please contact:
1-888-404-1388
www.goldtouchpress.com
book.orders@goldtouchpress.com

Printed in the United States of America

Contents

Ultimate Youth Lifestyle vii
Attack on Titan, a Masterpiece in the Making 1
The Art of Aesthetics 3
A Basic Guide to Thrifting 5
Astrology and How to Find your Big Three 7
Copy of 3 Ways to Hang Your Posters up 9
My Favorite Crystals 10
Fully Understanding a Book 11
How I Make Money as a Teen 12
Finding your Music taste 13
.How I handle a busy schedule 14
Learning a language - My Experiences and Tips 15
How to Study for a Test 16
How to Save Money while Shopping 17
The Trending K-Drama - Squid Game 18
My School Experience in China 19
My Morning, Night, Weekend Routine 20
Must Needs for Vocalists 21
Tips for Dye and Cutting Hair at Home 22
Tips on Starting to Dance 23
Travel Essentials 24
Travel Essentials - Part 2 25
Genshin Impact, the Mobile Game 26
Why Spirited Away is my Favorite Movie 28

What is Lucid Dreaming? 30
Hot Pot - Chinese Food 31
What to do in Quarantine When you're Bored 32
How to Start a Small Business... 33
How to Plan your Vacation 34
How to Become Famous on Social Media 35

Ultimate Youth Lifestyle

Yaxuan Yang

About Book -

A collection of articles written for the Tempus Magazine as an editor for the Lifestyle column. This features a number of articles - all with different topics. Read more to find out.

About author -

Yaxuan Elsa Yang is a 9th grade student at Millburn High School. She likes writing books including articles for the lifestyle column in the Tempus magazine - that inspired her to write this book!

Attack on Titan, a Masterpiece in the Making

"That day, humanity remembered, the terror of being ruled by them, the humiliation of being kept in a cage." Attack on Titan, first created in 2013 follows the protagonist, Eren Jeager and his struggles of a world dominated by titans, a race of giant, man-eating humanoids. As the story moves forward, it uncovers some unpleasant secrets regarding the outside of the unknown society.

The show itself is intriguing, it includes action packed scenes and covers intense character development, including different timelines from now. Attack on Titan features interesting characters. Each of them has their own storyline and everybody gets quality screen time. The plot twists are highly unpredictable, it's most likely not what you'd expect. One of the morals and outcomes of this show is that in order to achieve success and freedom, sacrifices have to be made.

The anime originated from a manga, created by Hajime Isayama, a Japanese manga artist, and the first chapter was released in 2009, in the Shōnen magazine. It was later animated and produced by WIT studios. It has 4 seasons in all, with the 4th season animated by MAPPA and still airing every Sunday at the moment. Currently, the manga has 138 chapters and 34 volumes. It is expected to finish on April 8th where the last chapter of this series will be released.

"I used to play a video game called MUV LUV ALTERNATIVE. It was about aliens taking over the earth and the human race reaching extinction." This was the inspiration to Isayama to create Attack On titan. Isayama stated how he wanted to express the raw anger of the victims of a tragedy and how it can drive people to aggression.

Unlike other anime, Attack on Titan features strong female leads and no weak female representation. During the show, your mind will be filled with questions and you will remain confused until all the questions are slowly answered and revealed one by one. The animation in the anime is intriguing, for example a scene in the anime had to take a month to animate because it was so complex.

With such a fascinating storyline, non anime watchers and anime watchers who haven't watched this anime should check it out before the ending of the manga comes out. I personally believe that Isayama Hajime, the author, will bring us an artistic and bittersweet ending for readers. The 12-year manga series will close to an end.

The Art of Aesthetics

Aesthetics, or esthetics are branches of philosophy that deal with the nature of beauty and taste, as well as the philosophy of art. Aesthetics are particularly popular amongst teenagers. For example, finding an aesthetic is like finding what vibe a person matches with. Aesthetics are visual trends, making one find their aesthetic is like that specific aesthetic representing the person in some sort of aspect, it can be their dressing style or they can just simply enjoy that aesthetic. There are many aesthetics but below are a few popular ones.

During the pandemic, the Cottagecore aesthetic blew up on social media including Tiktok and Tumblr. The Cottage Core aesthetic is inspired by the western agricultural life, and is typically centered around environment, food and caring. The keywords to this aesthetic, as stated in the Aesthetics Wikipedia are Cottages, farm animals, wild-flowers, pies, crops, and gingham. The key colors to this aesthetic are green, brown, yellow, and cream/off-white. The dressing style of this aesthetic include lace, pastel puffy dresses and hand-crafted accessories.The visuals of this aesthetic include fairies, pressed flowers, crowns, baking, forests, handwritten letters, etc. There are a lot more aesthetics related to this one aesthetic.

Dark Academia has always been a popular aesthetic. It centers around classic literature and a passion for learning and reading. Key motives and visuals include books, history, reading, literature, writing, mystery, art, museums, daggers, fountain pens, antique books, coffee and tea, newspaper and cafes, etc. The colors of this aesthetic are usually dark-ish earth tones, black, brown, tan. The clothing style for Dark Academia comes from old school uniforms, for example light blouses, sweater vests, pleated skirts, cardigans, blazers, simple rings, etc. Like Dark Academia, there are many more aesthetics surrounding the word 'academia", for example: Light Academia, Writer Academia, etc.

Another popular aesthetic includes Vaporwave, characterized by the other-extensive use of samples, put in a chaotic and distorted fashion. This aesthetic includes strong nostalgia from the 80s and 90s. It may include 3D graphics, old computer OS, marble statues and just a scientific look in general. The colors include neon colors involving pink, blue and purple. Aesthetics like these may also include the Y2K aesthetic. The Y2K aesthetic centers around the years 1995 to 2003.

There are unlimited aesthetics existing, one can even create their own aesthetic. If you wish to explore further more about aesthetics, you can google the aesthetics and gain more knowledge about them, or even try to find your own aesthetic.

A Basic Guide to Thrifting

Many people may struggle on finding clothes, furniture and items they need that are affordable and fit their style, and thrifting is the way to solve it. Now, many people may ask: What is thrifting? Well, thrifting is basically shopping at a thrift store. Thrifted items are usually owned by a previous owner but are in good shape to be owned by another owner. Thrifting items may include basically anything, from a variety of clothes to furniture to books and many more items. Customers are shopping around the store, finding what they like and trying it on, finally buying the item for a cheap and affordable price.

Now, many may ask: How do I find good deals at thrifting stores? It is said that when going to thrift, the best time to go is in the morning, when the thrift store has just opened. When going in the morning, you should head to the sections with furniture, bags and shoes first because they will be organized first thing in the morning. Going on weekdays is better than weekends because less people will be there with more items. Shopping for off season clothes can be great because the items will be much cheaper, for example in Winter, Springtime items will be cheaper and vice versa.

A great tip is that whenever you're looking for cool and stylish graphic t-shirts and oversized t-shirts, look in the men's section. It includes a huge selection of different shirts. There are a large amount of jeans in thrift stores, and honestly in my opinion, they are the most worth it. Vases are also a great thing to look out for when thrifting. They come in different sizes and shapes and they're very affordable.

Another tip is that when thrifting, take your time and look through section by section, this will make things much easier. When looking, look through each individual item, you'll never know what you can find.

Before going thrifting, a tip is to look for pictures of items you'd like to find. Great apps for inspiration are Pinterest, Tiktok, Tumblr and

Instagram. When you're looking for a specific item, it is way better than searching without a target item. When thrifting, don't always look for the clothes that look stylish and good, instead look for things that don't look that stylish and figure out how to style it will improve your thrifting experience.

Thrifting can be a great experience, but knowing HOW to thrift will make thrifting much easier and cheaper.

Astrology and How to Find your Big Three

Many people have a certain amount of knowledge on astrology, but there is a much deeper area surrounding it, and today's topic is surrounding your sun sign, moon sign and your ascendant, otherwise known as your rising. Now, people may ask: what is a sun sign, a moon sign and a rising sign? Well, these 3 signs help you gain a better understanding of yourself.

Your Sun sign is the most common sign that people know about, since it is based on your birth month and date. For example, my birthday is on the 28th of February, so that would make me a Pisces, which is my sun sign. You can find your sun sign by searching up your date of birth and seeing what sign that date falls under the category of. When people ask you what your zodiac is, you should tell them this, because it is common to know of. Your sun sign represents you, because the sun is the center of the solar system, related to earth.

Your Moon sign isn't as commonly known as your sun sign. Your moon sign revolves around how you feel, your emotions, fears...etc. Your moon sign is a side that stays hidden to people, just like when it's daytime, the sun rises up and the moon hides away. The moon sign is basically like showing yourself on a deeper level. To find your moon sign, you need to find out where the moon was when you were born. To calculate your moon sign, you will need your birthplace, birth date and exact birth time, just go on any browser and search up the moon sign calculator and it should tell you exactly what it is, along with a description of the traits.

Lastly is your Ascendant, otherwise known as your Rising sign. This sign is how you show yourself to other people, how you dress, what your personality is like around new people, and how you represent yourself. When meeting others for the first time, you're most likely to act like your rising sign, since it's like a mask. It's how you appear to other people. Same as the moon sign, you need your birthplace, birth date and exact birth time, search up rising sign calculator for more information.

These 3 signs are the basics of horoscopes, of course, there are more placements like your mercury sign, mars, venus, etc. You can look into that by searching up your birth chart, and it will show you a self you've never discovered before.

Copy of 3 Ways to Hang Your Posters up

In this article, I'll be telling you how to hang the posters that you have or want to hang up. The majority of us have posters at home, whether it's a character, a place, a thing that we've interested in. But the question is: what material can I use to hang the posters up without damaging them?

Well, one of the simple solutions is to use tape. Clear tape is very helpful in most situations - not this one. If you use clear tape to hang your poster, when you take it down the tape will rip with the poster, destroying it. So, a solution is to just simply use another type of tape, which I recommend painter's tape. Yes, judging the title, its tape used for painters to paint places on their canvas. This tape is easy to take down and work with and will not damage the poster.

Another option is to use magnets. Yes, magnets are another option. You may be wondering - how do I hang stuff up with magnets? They won't stick. It's simple. Use painter's tape and put the magnet on the back of the sticky side of the tape, then put it to the wall. Use another magnet, and another roll of tape, put another magnet against the poster, then, the magnets will attract and stick!

The last option is using a mounting putty. Mounting putty is like a hard putty which sticks onto surfaces. I feel like all of us have played with it before when we were children. Just put the putty on the wall and stick the poster against the wall. You can get it on amazon.

Above are all the ways on how I stick my posters on the wall. Of course, if you have more options feel free to use your way.

My Favorite Crystals

In the past, crystals were used as ancient forms of medicine, with different crystals used to uplift different energies. To simplify, it basically is a spiritual energy that can help you achieve a positive state of mind. Here are some of my favorite crystals and stones.

Walking into my local crystal store, the first one that catches my eye is always Rose Quartz. It is a pink colored quartz, also known as Hyaline quartz. Rose Quartz is the stone of love. It can be used to bring back peace and trust in friendships and is considered a healing stone. An example of using Rose Quartz is to put it around when you're meditating, or wearing a rose quartz necklace, keeping it close to your heart. Rose quartz was the first crystal I had ever gotten, I enjoy wearing it as a necklace.

Another of my personal favorites is Tiger's eye. It is a crystal with gold and brown to red colors with silky patterns. Tiger's eye is a stone of protection and can also be used to bring good luck. It allows the owner to resolve problems and is useful for healing too. I adore this crystal because its colors are beautiful and it is very useful as well. A way to benefit from this crystal is to wear it when sleeping, since it is said to have healing properties.

Citrine is also one of my favorites, not only because of its beautiful color, but also because of its benefits. Citrine is said to attract wealth and success, as well as joy, light and self-confidence. The stone itself symbolizes joy and can absorb negativity and reduce anxiety. Wearing citrine daily can capture its power.

There are many crystals in the world, but these are my personal favorites which have helped me. Feel free to research and find your favorite crystal.

Fully Understanding a Book

Hello, in this article I will be giving you tips on how to fully understand a book - the meaning, what it means in depth and what it's saying. Read furthermore to find out. Below are three tips to help you.

The first thing I like to do when I am reading the book is to annotate. I write down how I feel about certain events, characters and dialogue in the book. I also write down quotes I feel are interesting. I feel like this helps me understand the book better and more in depth. After I finish the book, I look back at my annotations and write down more thoughts.

Another thing that I like to do is look at the annotations of websites because they give me a better understanding. I like using sparknotes because it helps me a lot to understand what is going on with the story, especially when the story is hard to understand and the wording is unique. After that I can know what certain scenes are showing.

The last thing I like to do is talk about it to someone who has also read this book. This helps me understand what they're feeling and if they have different thoughts than me - which I'm happy to listen to. I like to engage in conversations with people who have read this book.

Above are my tips on how to understand a book better and understanding a book can be hard, especially if the wording is complicated.

How I Make Money as a Teen

Today I will be showing you how I made money as a teenager. I will be introducing 3 ways!

The first way - I like to make money by selling my old clothes. When I look in my closet, I find clothes that I do not need and will not wear again in the future. This indicates to me that I should sell them. The app I use is Depop. I just link my payment method, I start by introducing the item and setting a price, then setting up shipping and putting hashtags for people to discover it. Sometimes it takes a while for someone to be interested in it, but just be patient - it's worth it!

The second way - Commissions are a big thing. I like to draw and to voice act. I posted them and people discovered them, and I was introduced to commissions. Commissions are basically where someone pays you to draw, or voice them something of their choice. Then based on how long / advanced it is, they pay you. I find that this is very helpful and has gained me much money in my savings.

The third way - Etsy businesses are another way. I personally have not done this but one of my friends has. She has started a jewelry business and it has been going very well. She makes jewelry and customers buy them, she packs and ships them and her customers are very satisfied. She tells me, when selling items, do your research first. Look in the market and get inspiration. Look at the prices of the other business, and set a reasonable price for the thing you are selling. If your price is too high, people will not buy from you, if your price is too low, you will lose money.

After reading, I hope you have gained some knowledge on how me or my friends make money.

Finding your Music taste

There are many apps to stream music on, there are many songs that exist that are currently releasing every day. People have different music tastes, so I'm here to help you find your music taste.

I hope you have already listened to an amount of songs to find songs that you like. Personally, when I started trying to find what I like, I would make a playlist of songs that I liked, and I would put the songs in that playlist. Next, I would search up the genre of songs that I put in the playlist. Then, I would make a sheet of what genre of songs is the most in my playlist. Then, I would try to find songs that are in that genre and listen to them, if I liked it, then I would feel like that was one of the music genres I liked. I would also ask my friends what genres of music they like and get ideas from them

This is my story with different music genres. At first, I really liked soft songs and I would constantly listen to them to get comfort. Then, my taste eventually evolved to hype songs with rap in them. I liked both English songs and Korean songs. Pop was a favorite genre for me and I felt that my taste in music does change a lot according to your mood and growth. I also feel that music is very subjective so if you dislike something, another person might love it. I feel that you should not bash someone for what music they listen to because everyone has different music tastes.

I hope you learned from this article and I hope you can find your music genre very soon. Finding out your music taste takes time, don't rush it.

How I handle a busy schedule

Sometimes, having a busy week may be very stressful, but the reason is because there's so many things to do. Although this can't cancel the plans and the events, it can help you organize your week to make sure you have a week that goes smoothly.

The 1st thing I like to do, is after I flip my calendar to the next month, I use a marker to write all the dates that I have something in. This will ensure that I know what I'm doing each day, and if someone asks me a question about my schedule I can answer. I would also take a picture of it so I can have access to the schedule on my phone. This ensures I don't have to get the calendar out every 2 seconds.

The next thing to do is to plan out your free time. Your free time is limited, and that is why you need to exactly plan it out so you have enough time to work and to rest. I like to see how long my free time is, and divide it based on preference. It's really just personal preference, everyone prefers something but make sure you do actually have time to work - you don't want to not get anything done, and make sure you don't just work through your free time - you don't want to overwork yourself.

The last thing I would do is to mentally keep up with this. I know this may sound a little harsh but there's really nothing you could do but encourage and remind yourself about your schedule. Commit to the things and events - they will bring you good things in the future.

A busy schedule is one of the things I hate the most. Especially when I want to hang out with my friends but I'm very busy. I hope this article helped you and you take my advice!

Learning a language - My Experiences and Tips

A lot of us want to learn a new language, but sometimes it's just way too hard to dig into something that you don't know. Below are my experiences and what I recommend doing to learn a new language.

I had to learn English in second grade, I went to school and took an English class, and my English improved dramatically after talking with classmates and eventually learning the language from them. My teacher was also very nice, helping me to work on projects, write poems and stories, take speaking tests, and much more. What I noticed about learning language is that if you communicate with the people who speak the same language, you'll eventually get to know that language. Communication is important, it helps you a lot on your language journey.

When starting to learn a new language, you want to first research it because of the different types of writing or speaking. Then start learning the basics of the language, like grammar, the alphabet, how to say it, how to write it, etc. Don't just learn it by yourself because it'll be very difficult: search videos on it, ask people about it, get outside information. What I recommend is, if possible, taking some time and going to the country that speaks the language. By communicating with people that speak the language, you will learn a lot more than just using a random language app. Another tip is that when learning, don't just learn about how to speak it, or how to write it. Learn about the culture of the language, where it came, from who made it and more.

Sometimes, we all feel the urge to give up. But just remember, keep learning and you eventually will speak the language fluently.

How to Study for a Test

Studying can be annoying sometimes, but it is needed to pass a test. While it isn't easy, this guide may help you study and give you tips.

First thing you should do is try to study a week before the test, as soon as possible. Take your time to plan out what you're studying each day. By studying earlier, you have more time to review for the upcoming test and the more you can memorize all the facts you're being tested on.

Second thing is that you should bring out your notes and write them down and make flashcards. Making flashcards is a very efficient way to remember terms that you aren't familiar with. Writing what you have learned down in a Google document and summarizing all your notes can be especially useful, as it will help you by organizing your notes into one document.

Another thing if you want to fully memorize your notes, is to read them out loud to other people like you're performing on stage. What I like to do is take stuffed animals and use them as my audience, using my notes and deliver a speech to them about what I'm being tested on. I also like to repeat words and sentences in my head. I find this to be really efficient when it comes to memorizing a formula or some kind of fact.

Your surroundings are very important when it comes to studying. For me, I always try to find a quiet and clean space like the library. When I'm at my house, my room is messy so I feel annoyed and I don't want to concentrate on my studies. What I do is go to the library after school and study there, as it's very quiet and doesn't disrupt study sessions.

Everyone's studying methods are different, don't rush and take your time to find what is right for you. I wish you the best of luck on your test.

How to Save Money while Shopping

Sometimes, you go to friends and you get a little overboard with shopping. This is a guide and a few tips to help you save money while going out and shopping.

Before going out with a friend, you want to prepare a list of what you want to buy. By doing that, you know where to look and you know where to go. You also want to set a budget for what you're going to buy. This lets you ensure that you don't go overboard and spend all your money on this one thing you want. After paying, ask for receipts every time you purchase something so you can keep track of how much money you spend. I recommend getting apps that track how much money you spend each day so you can see your stats in one month.

Let's say for instance, you stumble across something you're really interested in. Do you want to ask yourself a question, do I really need it? Does it benefit my life? Is it worth the money? If you think it benefits your life and you really need it but it's way too expensive, it's possible that online websites will provide a similar thing that is closer to your budget.

When you see something you like, do not buy it just because it looks good or you like it. I have bought many things in the past just because I thought they were pretty, but were completely useless and now sit in the corner of my room. Do not waste your money on useless things that you will not use in the future, ask yourself a question, will you still be using this in the future?

I hope this helped you save money and buy less useless things on your next shopping trip!

The Trending K-Drama - Squid Game

Netflix has just released a South Korean survival drama series: Squid Game. Written and directed by Hwang Dong Hyuk and starring Lee Jung-Jae, it is trending on TikTok, Instagram, everywhere.

Squid Game debuted on September 17 and was an instant hit. The drama is about hundreds of cash-strapped players accepting an invitation to compete in children's games. A tempting prize awaits them, but danger awaits as well: failure to win the games results in death. Many people are recreating games from the drama, such as one scene, where contestants have to carve out the shape they were given on a special type of candy, Dalgona. On Tiktok, many people try to recreate the scene, some fail and some succeed. Not only that, people are selling related merch and Halloween costumes surrounding the topic as well. The intense action in each episode makes the audience sit on the edge of their seats, predicting what will happen next.

In my opinion, Squid Game is a well-made masterpiece, with plot twists and sad moments that made everyone tear up. Some of the characters are hated, and some of them are loved. The show has an 8.3 out of 10 on IMDb and 100% rotten tomatoes. On Google users, 97% of the users enjoyed this TV show as well. Squid game is ranked number one in the US just four days after its debut; more than 82 million subscribers have seen this in its first 28 days. Netflix did not expect this show to have this many viewer and for Squid Game to be this popular. The director of the show says, "I don't have developed plans for Squid Game 2. It is quite tiring just thinking about it. But if I were to do it, I would certainly not do it alone. I'd consider using a writers' room and multiple experienced directors."

If you like dystopian horror and action Korean dramas, or just TV shows in general, you should definitely give this a try.

My School Experience in China

Back in 2017, I went back to China to study 2 years in China. I felt like Chinese schools and American schools have different education systems and different people.

First thing I noticed is that schools in China are usually stricter than schools in America. American schools allow piercings, dyed hair, hair down, but schools in China do not allow piercings, any dyed hair, and require students' hair to be tied up.

I also noticed that the lunches are different. In America, you pay to get different kinds of lunches but back in my elementary school in China, we would only have 1 option for lunch and it was a box with food, rice, and a soup. Back then we also did not have a cafeteria so we had to get in our own classrooms which I did not enjoy.

I also noticed how classes are longer than schools In America. We would have 4-minute breaks and we would go to class after In the same classroom. Right now, I'm In high school, and throughout middle school and high school I found that we had to go to different classrooms for teachers. In China, the teachers would come to us, which is the opposite from America.

Teachers are stricter than teachers in America. They gave out tests and no quizzes that were all worth 100 points. Luckily, my teachers were understanding and they knew I had trouble speaking Chinese so they helped me with a lot of things. I am very grateful for having these teachers.

Of course, there are many more differences than just those, but I cannot include all of them in one article. If you would like to know more, you can do a quick research on the internet to find out more differences about classes, people, clubs and more.

My Morning, Night, Weekend Routine

Hi, I'd like to show you my everyday routines that I do, and I hope you can get inspiration from me as well.

First, I like to start by introducing my night routine. After I finish my homework, I pack my backpack and go shower. After I shower, when it is the weekend, I like to put on a face mask and go on my phone for a while. I look around and chat with friends until I wash the face mask off and put on skin products I like to use. After that, I go to bed and read, and I sleep. I usually sleep around 11 pm, I do have a lot of work sometimes and that is a reasonable time in my opinion.

Next, I will introduce my morning routine. When I wake up, I start by washing my face. Then, I put on the products I use and start doing my makeup. I usually only use eyeliner and eyeshadow. After that, I started changing schools. I always spent quite some time picking my outfits. Then I start going downstairs for breakfast. When I'm eating breakfast, I think about if I missed any work. After eating breakfast, I grab my bags and head to school. My school is very close to my house so I usually walk there.

Lastly, I will briefly explain what I do on the weekends. On Friday, I will try to get all my work done. On Saturday, I hang out with friends and go to places and have fun. On Sunday, I have classes, but after that I can relax in the night and do whatever I want.

I hope this helped you in some way if you're also trying to devise a healthy routine. A healthy routine is the start to a healthy day.

Must Needs for Vocalists

You probably clicked on this article because you want to be a singer and start making music. Well, here are a few essential-must-needs for you and your journey.

When you listen to a song, what do you notice? Something I've always noticed is how all songs don't have background noise, I think all of us know that they use one thing to fix that - a microphone. Having a good microphone ensures your audio quality is top tier - when I got my first microphone the sound quality on the things I recorded drastically and I was very happy. One microphone I recommend is the Blue Yeti, which is very well known in microphone selections - it's on the pricey side but it's very worth it.

Another thing that is essential for vocalists are apps/installments to make the voices blend. One installment I recommend is Garageband. Garageband is very helpful if you want to record and make songs because it provides a lot of settings you can play around with, if you're interested you can look into it further.

Last thing I recommend is having a platform to upload music on. Try to start with a base - start posting before you even have music - this gives you a base before you start your actual career. Any social media works but the 2 I recommend are Youtube and Tiktok.

I hope you learned something and take my advice too. Thanks for reading and I wish you best of luck on your journey.

Tips for Dye and Cutting Hair at Home

In the past, I have had many experiences with hair. I have cut hair, dyed hair, and bleached hair at home. This is a guide on how to not mess up.

First, are dyeing tips. Brands are very important. I do not recommend box dye because it can damage your hair. Instead, do research on the internet for good brands of dye. For bleach, I recommend the L'Oréal Quick Blue Powder Bleach. Picking the right brand of bleach is very important too. It is a big factor in causing your hair to be dead. When dyeing hair, do not do it by yourself. Either call a friend or a family member to help you. Start by doing strands on your head, and do the top of your head last because it absorbs the bleach more quickly. Ask the person dying your hair to apply bleach/dye evenly. When I dyed my hair, my friend and I did not apply it evenly enough, and it caused clumps of color in my hair.

Next is cutting hair. I cut my hair almost every week out of impulse, but do not be like me. If you wanna cut your hair shorter, make sure to cut them to the same length. But that is not the hard part, the hard part is cutting bangs. Scrolling through social media, I always see people cutting their own bangs and it always goes very well or very wrong. Make sure you don't cut it too short if you're cutting actual bangs, cut it to your eyes. If you're cutting curtain bangs, do not cut straight onto your hair. Cut layers. I recommend going to a salon if you're cutting bangs to get professionally done.

Hair is a major factor that can affect your appearance and style. If you can, please go to a salon to dye or cut your hair. If you really want to dye it yourself, follow the tips above.

Tips on Starting to Dance

As someone who is currently learning different kinds and styles of dance, I have learned quite a lot from my experiences. Below are my tips of what I recommend doing and not doing.

First, dancing is something I recommend practicing a lot for. One time, I learned a new dance but I did not practice it a lot. Later when I went to my class to review and learn the next part, I found that I had trouble doing all the parts and that led to me struggling to keep up with the teacher. Spend some time each day to review so you don't forget.

Next, if you don't understand something, immediately go to the teacher and ask them for advice. The most important part of learning is asking questions. I like to wait until the end of the class and go up to them to ask for any tips they want to give me. This ensures that I can learn the proper moves and be able to perform nicely. One experience personally is when we learned a new part I did not understand a part so I went to the teacher to ask her. She explained everything nicely and I understood immediately after.

Lastly, I recommend looking at yourself or getting a mirror, or record yourself when you practice. Sometimes, you might think you're doing the moves right but when you look at yourself in the mirror, or recording yourself you look completely different and wrong. I like to get a phone out and record myself when I practice so I can see what I did wrong and fix my moves. I found this to be very important and needed.

Above is what I recommend doing, with this I personally did much better in my journey. I hope you learn something from it.

Travel Essentials

In this article, I'll be telling you some things I recommend bringing on a trip with you. These items will help you on the way and ensure that you have a great time.

"I always bring a small container of laundry detergent so I can hand-wash clothes in the sink. If I can do laundry on-the-go, I don't have to pack as many outfits." —Nikki G, 34, a travel blogger who takes four or five international trips and one or two domestic trips each year. These on the go laundry detergents are easy to carry and fits perfectly in a bag or suitcase. Whenever you need to wash clothes, you can just open this laundry detergent and start washing your clothes immediately. For 6 packs it is $19.

Portable hotspot and wifi are essential things you need to bring on your trip. Say you're at a place with no wifi, you can just open the hotspot/wifi and it will work just like magic. Say you're working on your computer, and you don't have wifi. This will help you a lot. A GlobalMe mobile hotspot is $165.

Battery operated fans are also a key for going on trips in the summer. Say you're going to a place where it can get very hot sometimes, and nothing is gonna help you relieve the heat, but this fan. I saw some that also came with a flashlight so at night it can help you see better. For a battery-operated fan, it is $14.

Here are just some of the travel essentials I recommend. I have many more I'd love to share in the future, but I hope this article helped you and your travel. In the future, I will be making a continued version of this because there are just too many items I'd like to share.

Travel Essentials - Part 2

In the last article, I mentioned a few of my favorite travel essentials, and now I am here to share some more that I have personally tested and tried out for myself. All of these are my honest experiences and reviews.

The first thing I'd recommend you do if you're going on an airplane for a long period of time is getting a sleep mask. A silk one, to be exact. Silk sleeping masks are very soft, smooth and silky, ensuring you a great sleep and a great dream. You will not wake up with lines on your face unlike the airline ones, which in my opinion are very uncomfortable.

The next thing I recommend is actually entertainment wise, or rather something to pass the time with. And with that, I'd like to introduce the Kindle. When I was very young, I used to own a kindle and read all kinds of books I liked. Now my kindle is sitting in my drawer and I plan to use it on my next trip. A kindle is better than a book in many ways - you can still read it if it's dark, you can read multiple books on one device, etc.

The last thing I recommend is getting a first aid kit. Not to scare you, but incidents could happen on the trip that are unexpected, and the last thing you want is being unprepared and panicking about that. A good one I found was Welly's Human Repair kit, which includes basics of disinfecting injuries. This won't help you make the injury smaller, but it might help you stop the bleeding.

I hope this article can help you and show you many products you'd need on your next journey. If you have any questions, feel free to comment down below and ask for the links of these products.

Genshin Impact, the Mobile Game

"Embark on a journey across Teyvat to find your lost sibling and seek answers from The Seven — the gods of each element." Genshin Impact, a multiplayer open world game has gotten quite popular in the past few months. Many players are attracted to the storyline, the characters and the scenery.

In the game Genshin Impact, it features 2 main characters, Aether and Lumine, twins who have traveled across many worlds but one day being separated by an unknown god. Players have the choice to select a twin to be the character they're going to play as. (The storyline has no relation to which twin you pick.) You find yourself in the land of Teyvat. You find statues of different elements, as you explore the world and try to find your twin. If that sounded intriguing to you, give the game a try.

As mentioned in the first paragraph, many players enjoy it because of the characters, not just because of the storyline. In Genshin Impact, there are more than 30 characters you can have and play as. Each has their unique character design and they have an element out of the 6: Geo (earth), Electro (lightning) Pyro (fire), Cryo (ice), Anemo (wind), and Dendro (nature). Each character also has their own storyline and you can explore that while playing the game. Popular characters may include Kaeya, Diluc, Xiao, Zhongli, etc.

Genshin Impact's scenery deserves an award. Despite it being a Mobile game, its scenery is beautiful and realistic. It also runs on a PC, which is much smoother than a phone. There are seven nations in Genshin: Mondstadt, Liyue,

Inazuma, Sumeru, Fontaine, Natlan, and Snezhnaya, each being ruled by a god. You can climb any mountain, talk to any NPC (Non-player character), you could swim across lakes and investigate every inch of the world. The art style is gorgeous, weather can change anytime, there is real time rendering and the character's animations make everything come alive. The soundtrack is performed by the London Philharmonic Orchestra, it changes overtime when you enter different areas and encounter different creatures.

Yaxuan Elsa Yang

Why Spirited Away is my Favorite Movie

Growing up, one of my favorite activities to do was to sit in the movie theaters and watch movies. I always loved staring at a big screen in the dark, watching a movie that caught my attention. I have watched a great amount of movies, but my favorite out of all of them is Spirited Away.

Spirited Away follows a child by the name of Chihiro and her parents moving to a new home. They stumble across an abandoned field of some sort and find food vendors filled with food, which her parents eat and become pigs. When she tries to find her way back, she notices that the other side of the field was separated by a lake. She sees a hotel of some sort and meets a guy named Haku, who tells her that this place is a stopping place for spirits to stay when they are tired from spending time in the earthly realm.

The main reason that I like this movie is because of its amazing animation, along with the voice acting that brings it all together. It is an animated movie, its production company is Studio Ghibli which is a popular company that also produced Howl's Moving Castle, My Neighbor Totoro, etc. The movie creates a gorgeous art style and fancy scenery. The voice acting is in Japanese and personally I feel like they put a lot of emotion into their parts. Another reason why I like this movie is because of its plot. It is a fantasy and a coming of age story, and it also has a lot of action. I have watched this movie about 4 times and I still want to watch it again. The characters are well written and have a lot of character development.

Spirited Away was released in 2001 in Japan, but I watched it in theaters in 2018. It has gotten an 8.6 and It has a runtime of 2 hours and 5 minutes. The movie does not include any mature scenes so you can watch it with family and friends.

This movie won the Academy Award for Best animated feature at the 75th Academy Awards, which makes it the First Non-English Animated Film to win the award. It has also won the Golden Bear in 2002. If you are interested in what I have just recommended, go check this movie out yourself.

What is Lucid Dreaming?

A lucid dream is where the dreamer becomes aware of the fact that they are dreaming. The dreamer can gain control of their dream.

Where does lucid dreaming come from - the reason for lucid dream may come from overcoming fears, healing, wish fulfillment, according to the sleep foundation.

Health line mentions: "Lucid dreaming is when you're conscious during a dream. This typically happens during rapid eye movement (REM) sleep, the dream-stage of sleep. An estimated 55% of people have had one or more lucid dreams in their lifetime." Lucid dreaming lets you control what happens in your dream. Dr. Stephen LaBerge is a very popular researcher in the lucid dreaming field. One of his techniques was his invention. "In 1980, LaBerge created a technique called Mnemonic Induction of Lucid Dreams (MILD). It was one of the first methods that used scientific research to induce lucid dreams. MILD is based on a behavior called prospective memory, which involves setting an intention to do something later." Is what healthline mentioned.

How to lucid dream? - there are a few tips. Reality testing is one. Reality testing is a form of mental training. It trains your mind to take notice of your awareness. During the day, take time to ask yourself questions like Am I dreaming? Or count how many fingers you have. Next, set an alarm 5 hours after your bedtime and go to sleep. When the alarm goes off, get up and stay up for 30 minutes, do a quiet activity and go back to sleep. In that dream, do reality checks like counting your fingers, being aware of your surroundings, etc. Affirmations are also a good way. Affirm that you lucid dreamed last night.

I hope you gained a good understanding of lucid dreaming, and if you're interested in knowing more, search it up on the internet.

Hot Pot - Chinese Food

As someone who travels to China every summer, there are a lot of foods that I have tasted. Based on my experience, this is my favorite food that I recommend you try when you visit China.

When visiting China, me, my mom, dad and my sister would go visit my cousins and grandparents. We always go out to eat different kinds of food, but Hot Pot is one of our favorites. Now you might ask, what is a Hot Pot? Well, it is an interactive meal where there is a pot of soup stock at the dining table with East Asian foods, ready to be cooked. It is a main dish and its Chinese name is called "Huoguo."

Hot Pot ingredients may include thin meat, vegetables, mushrooms, tofu, bean products, seafood, and basically anything you want to eat. By placing it in the soup, waiting for it to be cooked and then taking it out, dipping it in the sauces prepared for you, taking a bite brings satisfaction. Different ingredients have different cook times, and most raw foods can be cooked in a hot pot, some must be removed accordingly by time.

Hot Pot originated from the tripods of the Zhou dynasty. Empress Dowager Cixi was known to enjoy hot pot, along with Qianlong Emperor who was very fond of it and Jiaqing Emperor who had a banquet with 1,550 hot pots at his coronation.

Hot pot meals can enhance friendship and unite families because several people sit around the pot, talking, it makes people feel relaxed and it is very popular in winter and in cold places, since the hot pot itself is warm.

Hot Pot is extremely popular among Chinese foods and it is a must have when visiting China, it has become the major attraction of the tourism industry in some areas, go try it out for yourself.

What to do in Quarantine When you're Bored

During quarantine we were forced to stay inside, and my personal experience wasn't the best. I had to stay home, all I could do was look at my phone and go to class. Here are a few things that I recommend doing during quarantine that could help you and make your life better, and easier.

The first thing I recommend doing is making a diary for yourself. I think this is a really nice method to record your life in quarantine and also make your life fun. You can decorate the diary however you'd like to write whatever you want and draw whatever you want as well. When you realize it, a few hours will probably go by and this would be a really fun activity to do.

The next thing I recommend doing is playing games online and FaceTime with your friends. As we all know, when you're with your friends you are much happier and less bored. What you could do is you could FaceTime your friends and you could play games online while FaceTime. You could talk about the game and chitchat like you guys are in person.

The last thing I recommend doing is cooking or baking something for your family. The reason why I think this is an effective method to spend time during quarantine is first, time passes really easily by making things for your family to eat, and second your relationship with your family will improve over time. your cooking skills will improve dramatically as well!

Quarantine can be hard sometimes but with activities that would make a quarantine life easier and less boring, I think this would be a great time to spend more time with your family in the house, and your friends online. So, go ahead and try these activities for yourself.

How to Start a Small Business

Scrolling through TikTok I always see small business owners making TikToks about their small businesses. Today I'm going to give tips on how to start a small business based on my own experience.

The first thing you should do is find a suitable name for your small business. The name can't be too long or can't be too short. I recommend making it something you really like or something around your name. After you found that you should make a logo for a small business. If you can't draw, you can ask friends to do it for you, or you can hire someone to draw for you and pay them.

The next thing you should decide is what you're going to sell. On TikTok I see many small business owners selling lip glosses, lip tints and body scrubs, so that is a suggestion, however you can sell anything you want. When you decide to sell something, you want to take the picture clearly and in good lighting. People don't want to see the pictures in dark lighting or not from a good angle. The title should be a conclusion of what you're selling, and in the description, it should conclude what this product does and how to use it.

The last thing is where to sell it. You can really sell it wherever you want, but most small business owners sell it on Etsy, just register an account and start a shop. It's very simple. You can also make your own website. When you start your shop, don't expect people to go and buy your item immediately. You should post on social media about your products. Social media include Instagram, TikTok, Twitter or whatever platform you want to post on.

Starting a small business can be hard sometimes, but with help and support, I believe that your small business will get attention one day.

How to Plan your Vacation

Traveling can be very fun, but it also can be confusing if you don't have a plan. Based on my past travel experiences, I will provide details and ideas on how to provide a travel plan when you travel.

First, I would suggest researching the place you're going to. For example, searching up the city, the town, sight-seeing places would be a great advantage to your vacation. Find places you're interested in, when they open, how much the admission fee costs, parking, nearby restaurants, and more. This will ensure that when you go to the place you want to go; it won't be awkward when you arrive and leave. One time, I was in New York, and we didn't notice that we parked in the wrong place so we got a ticket. That was not pleasant.

Next, is to construct a route you're taking. If you're going to travel by a car, make sure you bring a map or GPS. If you're traveling by plane or train, ensure when your flight or when your train leaves. Arrive early and pack your things the night before. After you arrive, make sure to think of a transportation method to the hotel or the house you're heading to. Otherwise, you would spend much more time with that at the airport and waste a lot of time.

Lastly, I would suggest getting a planner or a calendar. Planning beforehand, write down the dates and which date you're going to which place to ensure that you know where you're going and waste less time. One of my previous experiences is not planning out what time to go where. That resulted in me staying at the hotel for most of the day.

Going on a trip is a really fun experience, most of my past experiences have been fun and successful with a plan. I recommend you to start planning for the future. It really helps a lot.

How to Become Famous on Social Media

Becoming famous is hard, but in the past, I have been successful with this topic. These are a few tips I recommend and tell you, when you want to become famous on social media sites like Tiktok and Instagram.

The first thing I did was create an account; on any social media I chose TikTok. The reason why I chose TikTok was because it was very popular and many people watched it. It was also because you can only make up to about 15 seconds in a video so you don't have to worry about the length. I made a catchy username that suited my account. That was basically it, I started posting videos.

When you post videos, you should find a topic and stick to the topic. This will make your followers watch your videos more often because they like the topic as well. When you post a video, make sure you put hashtags so people can find the video. The video can't be too short because people will scroll away once they think they're not interested in it. When you post one video, people aren't going to like your videos and follow you immediately because you just started. If you post more videos, then more and more people will find you and follow you. Don't have high expectations for all of your videos to get the same amount of high numbered likes. Some will, some will not.

My personal experience is that I made a TikTok account a while ago, and I posted a few videos until one got 190k likes. It was because I posted videos around the same topic, put a lot of hashtags, and kept posting videos. Now I have a few thousand followers on that account and I keep posting daily, or weekly.

Getting famous and liked can be hard sometimes, but it takes time. Posting more videos may help you a lot on your journey. Do not ever give up and keep trying.

www.ingramcontent.com/pod-product-compliance
Lightning Source LLC
Chambersburg PA
CBHW061103050726
47592CB00004B/1804

* 9 7 8 1 9 5 7 5 7 5 7 4 2 *